Professor Birdsong's

Dumbest Thieves, Thugs, & Rogues

Leonard Birdsong

Professor Birdsong's Dumbest: Thieves, Thugs, and Rogues
by Leonard Birdsong
© 2016 Leonard Birdsong
ISBN: 978-0-9898452-8-1

Winghurst Publications
1969 S. Alafaya Trail / Suite 303
Orlando, FL 32828-8732
www.BirdsongsLaw.com
lbirdsong@barry.edu

Permissions:
Cover graphics: ©Khalid S. Birdsong /
http:friedchickenandsushi.com
Book cover design: Rik Feeney / www.RickFeeney.com

Table of Contents

Introduction

Law Professor Leonard Birdsong lives in Florida where he teaches Criminal Law, Evidence, and Immigration Law. He has written many scholarly legal pieces since joining the legal academy.

Among his scholarly pieces are his books and articles entitled: *Immigration: Obama Must Act Now!*; *Felony Murder: A Historical Perspective by Which to Understand Today's Modern Felony Murder Rule Statutes; Comity and Our Federalism In The Twenty First Century: The Abstention Doctrines Will Always Be With Us - Get Over It!;* and *The Exclusion of Hearsay Through Forfeiture By Wrongdoing Old Wine In a New Bottle: Codification of the Concept Into Rule 804(b)(6).*

This is not one of those scholarly pieces!

This volume of Professor Birdsong's

Dumbest Criminal Stories: Thieves, Thugs & Rogues is written just for fun and enjoyment. It showcases stories from all over the world and contains the kind of many dumb, funny and weird criminal law stories that he has found and written about since 2010. Read them. Laugh at the stories and then go to Amazon.com and chose from his other inexpensive fourteen humor books for more such laughs. There are two series: *Professor Birdsong's Dumbest Criminal Stories* and *Professor Birdsong's Weird Criminal Law Stories.* As a matter of fact, you may find all of these other volumes at Amazon.com or by going to his website: LeonardBirdsong.com.

Some of you may criticize Professor Birdsong's editing of several of the stories that appear here, but be aware that Professor Birdsong attempts to report the stories herein as they may have appeared in police reports and news reports that appeared in the public domain without changing the original story. Professor Birdsong consulted *The New Oxford American Dictionary* (2d ed. 2005, Oxford Press) for his definitions concerning Thieves, Thugs and Rogues.

Enjoy the stories and have a few good laughs for my sake.

Chapter One
Thieves

This first chapter is devoted to thieves. As you already know the word thieves is the plural of the word thief. A thief is defined as a person who steals another's property, especially by stealth and without using force or violence. The origins of the word thief as we know it today comes from the old English word "thiof" which meant one who steals. The Old English word is close in origin to the Dutch word "dief" which means one who steals, as well as the German word "dieb," which also means to steal.

In today's America the word robber and thief are often used interchangeably. The real difference at law between the two is that robbery is generally accomplished by force or threat of force.

Just about everyone in the world learns the meaning of theft before they enter kindergarten. Now with this knowledge feast your eyes on these stories of dumb thieves and get your laugh on.

ARIZONA: *Right back to jail you go, you idiot!* A Phoenix man just released from county jail on drug charges ran laps around the facility to celebrate his freedom – then tried to carjack a truck belonging to the jail, police said. He was arrested when police saw him on surveillance cameras trying to start a marked truck parked at the jails loading dock.

CALIFORNIA: *MEOW...* A suspected car thief was chased to the third floor of a building and dangled out the window, threatening to commit suicide...until his cat came to the rescue according to San Francisco police. During the standoff, a relative of the suspect brought his orange tabby to the scene. The kitty's presence calmed the suspect and allowed police to talk him down.

CALIFORNIA: *The thief does not have a leg to stand on!* In LA a human leg was stolen from a van belonging to an organ-

and–tissue-donation organization, authorities report. The theft early on a Monday morning while staffers for the non-profit One Legacy stopped for a bite at a downtown restaurant. Police said the thief who stole the cooler in which the leg was stored didn't likely know what was in it, and was probably very surprised when he did look.

COLORADO: *What a dummy!!* Police in Colorado Springs tracked down house-break suspect Paul Gonzalez by simply following his footprints in the snow. Police quickly found the dummy who was actually surprised that lawmen had tracked him down with so little effort.

FLORIDA: *It appears he was dead wrong.* A Miami man was arrested for stealing a corpse from a casket. Pedro Gonzalez, 39, faces burglary charges after he allegedly broke into the Charlotte Jane Memorial Park Cemetery in Coconut Grove last year, yanked open a coffin and took the remains inside, said police. No one knows why Gonzalez wanted the corpse.

FLORIDA: Jacksonville police say Brian Jeffers stole $200 in a holdup at a sandwich shop. The shop was next door to a convenience store where Jeffers had borrowed $3 from a clerk. He was arrested when he returned to the convenience store to repay the $3 debt with the stolen money.

FLORIDA: *So how long have you had that headache, mister?* A bandit in Orlando broke into a convenience store by literally bashing in the front door with his head. The hardheaded crook shattered the glass at the sunshine Food Mart in Orlando and made off with $10,000 worth of scratch-off lottery tickets. The owner of the mart immediately contacted the Florida Lottery Commission and all the scratch-off tickets were cancelled before any could be used.

FLORIDA: *Gone in 60 seconds…* After a teen was sentenced to probation for auto theft, he left the court house with a sheath of legal papers. Those same documents were later found by police in the front seat of a stolen car. When St. Petersburg officers called the young man to arrange for him to pick up the court papers, he showed up in what? Yep another stolen car! He was ultimately arrested for theft of both cars.

FLORIDA: *The headline read: "Save the stuffing for Thanksgiving."* A man named Alto Blocker was caught with 19 cans of Vienna sausages, five cans of Spam, four bags of peanuts and two bottles of Vodka stuffed down his pants after leaving a Fort Pierce truck stop. He was pulled over by highway patrol officers a short time later. We learn that the total value of the stolen goods was $68.10.

FLORIDA: *What a moron!* A paraplegic allegedly stole a vehicle from an Ocala auto dealership by lifting himself inside a vehicle and working the gas and brake with his cane. The handicapped thief then led police on a brief chase that allowed him to outrun the police. He was arrested hours later at a gas station.

GEORGIA: *The headline for this one read: "What a panty waste."* A woman stole 785 pairs of sexy underwear at a Victoria's Secret Valentine's Day sale at an Atlanta mall. The bandit stuffed $10,000 worth of garments into three shopping bags and bolted from the store. She was seen on video wearing a red hat and tennis shoes – appropriate for Valentine's Day.

KANSAS: *Always chew your food thoroughly when stealing it!* It has been reported that a 48-year-old man nearly choked to death in a Wichita Mexican restaurant when he barged in, ran to the buffet counter and started shoving handfuls of hot pork into his mouth. He began choking and was rushed to a local hospital where medical personnel saved his life. Nevertheless, police say theft charges will be pursued against the man.

ILLINOIS: *The headline read: "His getaway car got away."* Che Hearn, 25, who lives in the town of Zion, has been nicknamed the "unlucky thief" after his car was repossessed during an alleged theft. A repo man towed Hearn's car while he was allegedly stealing electronics from a Walmart in Round Lake Beach, police report. We learn further that Hearn ditched the stolen goods when confronted by a store employee. He was later found walking on the side of the road and arrested.

ILLINOIS: *This fellow was indeed a dunce of a criminal.* A thief in Chicago was seen on video last year breaking a tavern's door lock, then tugging futilely on the door handle for 10 minutes trying to enter. Perhaps, just perhaps, he was a little too anxious or perhaps he couldn't read the sign on the door which read: "push to open." After ten minutes of silliness he fled the scene.

ILLINOIS: *Did they charge the kid as an aider and abettor?* An Illinois woman robbing a bank brought along her five year old son, police report. Lauri Ruble was charged with armed robbery of the Wauconda Community Bank while clutching her son in one hand and a butcher knife in the other hand. Ruble got away with $4,800, police report. However, she was arrested and faces criminal charges while also being investigated by the Department of Children and Family Services.

ILLINOIS: *What an idiot!!* A Chicago man was arrested for robbing a bank after he tried to deposit some of the dye-stained cash in another bank. The man had made off with over $5,000, but the cash was ruined when the dye-pack that the tellers stuffed in the bag exploded. He now faces federal bank robbery charges.

ILLINOIS: *A real lunkhead!* A Chicago man jumped behind the wheel of an ambulance and drove off as two paramedics worked on one of his relatives in the back. Jimmy McCoy, 27, might have thought he was helping out when he drove the ambulance as his family member was being treated for a diabetic episode. Lifesaver or not, McCoy was charged with unlawful possession of a stolen vehicle.

ILLINOIS *Father, you are going straight to hell with this type of conduct....* He may have missed this class in the seminary. A Roman Catholic priest was arrested for stealing butter and a sofa cover from an Illinois Wal-Mart. The Rev. Steven Poole also switched the price tag on a memory-foam mattress and pocketed a laptop power pack police said. Police said, "at least he'll have something to talk about in confession."

ILLINOIS: *Happy Birthday to you, Idiot!* Eager to buy himself a present on his 19th birthday, Michael Wells Jr. chose an unusual way to spend the day -- he tried to break into a Naperville home. DuPage county prosecutors say Wells' May 13, 2009, plans included selling what he stole for money get himself a birthday present. His plans were ruined when he was arrested by sheriff deputies during the break-in. He was sentenced to six months in jail after pleading guilty to attempted burglary. It appears that the only gift

Wells got for his birthday was the fact that the judge sentenced him to only six months instead of the five years sought by the prosecution.

ILLINOIS: *Sounds like someone should have called the "fashion police."* Three armed, masked men barged into a Chicago home a week after Christmas 2009, and forced 11 people to take off their pants. They then shot one of the victims in the leg. The robbers then fled with the pants and televisions. Police speculated that the pants were stolen in order to get the victims' wallets and to prevent them from chasing the robbers.

IOWA: *He was a real fraud, but the sentence is real!* We learn that Eddie Tipton, a former Iowa lottery official, was sentenced to ten years in prison for rigging a computerized game in 2010 in an attempt to win a $14 million jackpot. Mr. Tipton, 52, never received any money, and a jury convicted him in 2015 on two counts of fraud. He was also accused of trying to get friends to cash the prize for him without revealing his identity.

LOUISIANA: *Big stink???* It has been reported that Police in New Orleans are trying to sniff out a bad guy. He is a thief that stole 30 air fresheners from a Family Dollar Store, worth more than $200. It is obvious that the police would make a big stink over this case because there is a reward of $2,500 for information leading to the thief's arrest.

MARYLAND: *What a doofuss!* Robert Wilson, 42, bungled his bank robbery attempt horribly a few weeks ago when he dropped more than $20,000 he stole on the floor of the bank. He struggled to collect the cash in an upturned umbrella – then slipped on an icy sidewalk as he fled, cutting his head open. By the time he got to his getaway car, police were already in pursuit. They soon captured and arrested him. He is on his way to federal prison.

MICHIGAN: *Yep, gone in 60 seconds....* Did you ever hear the news that Detroit is a tough place? Here's confirmation. A few years ago, someone stole the tires off the car of one of the vehicles from, then Mayor Dave Bing's, entourage while it was parked at a condominium complex. "It is a microcosm of a larger challenge that we all have the responsibility of addressing," said a spokesperson for the Mayor's office.

MINNESOTA: *That was one well defended play fort!* Police Chief Eric Swenson of Sebeka reported that stun grenades, gas shotgun rounds, magazines loaded with pistol and rifle bullets, and a pair of night vision goggles had been stolen from his home. The red faced chief notified police authorities two days later that the mystery had been solved. His children had taken the lethal weapons to their home made built backyard play fort.

MINNESOTA: *Those must have been some really big pants!* A suburban Minneapolis man managed to walk out of a store with a 19 inch TV shoved down his pants. He also had a remote control for the TV, power cords and a bottle of brake fluid in his pants. Eric Lee King, 21, was caught when a police officer saw him drop a box of candy in the parking lot. The officer realized that King was walking strangely and at the same time he was trying to hold up his pants.

MINNESOTA: *The headline to this one could have read" "This crime was jug of bull."* A bandit stole $70,000 worth of bull semen from a farm in LeRoy. It appears that a storage unit in the farm's milking parlor was left unlocked, allowing the still at large thief to swipe the valuable material. Perhaps it was an inside job.

MISSOURI: *Perhaps he was really paving his highway to heaven.* A man apologized for building a patio out of the gravestones of dead war veterans. The unidentified homeowner in Ozark County said he got the gravestones from a nearby landfill after they were abandoned by a local monument maker. "I was just making something out of nothing. Ninety percent of them are broken. They were never in a cemetery," he said, adding that he plans to dismantle the patio.

NEW JERSEY: *A really creepy and desperate school bus aide.* A former school bus aide accused of taking lunch money and bagged lunches from preschoolers in the town of Millville has now also been charged with stealing cash from the bus driver. Rosa Rios, 33, was charged in March with additional theft and robbery counts. Police report that the new charges came after Rios had been earlier caught on a surveillance camera rummaging through students' backpacks. She was originally only accused of stealing money and food from the 3-to-5-year-olds she was supervising in January and February.

NEW MEXICO: *Oh, how quickly can the worm turns…* An awkward thief found himself getting "held up" at gunpoint after his victims cornered him with their possessions in his car. We learn that when Albuquerque police arrived they found a 66-year-old woman and her 70-year-old husband both pointing guns at the man who had allegedly burglarized their home and tried to make off with their belongings. The police revealed that 26-year-old Aaron Lujan had been released from jail one day earlier.

NEW YORK CITY: *The report says that a note-passing bank robber who's a sucker for sweets escaped with more than money.* On his way out of the bank, he paused near the door and helped himself to one of the lollipops the bank keeps on hand for customer with children. We assume that the suspect, Jonathan Boston, also sucked as a robber for he was caught soon after the stickup with the loot and the lollipop.

NEW YORK CITY: *Can we say the suspect was bottled up?* A dumb crook on the Lower East Side of Manhattan ducked under a liquor store's electronic security gate as it was closing – sealing him in the store until police arrived. Jermal James, 28, was discovered in the liquor store one Monday night in August, according to the criminal complaint. It appears that James had ducked under the gate as the owner was locking up for the night. With the lights off and nowhere to go, James pulled $2,100 from the register and $18 worth of alcohol from the shelf. However, fleeing with the loot was not an option because when the gate closed behind him the store was automatically locked moments after he had entered.

When police did arrive a few hours later James was arrested for burglary.

NEW YORK CITY: *Three true dummies and losers plead guilty.* Three Brooklyn men charged in a plot to join ISIS, kill President Obama, and bomb Coney Island pleaded not guilty in Mid-March 2015 in Brooklyn federal court. Just before trial Abror Habibov, 30, Akhror Saidakhmetov, 19, and Abdurasul Hasanovich, 24, all suddenly and sullenly changed their not guilty pleas and entered their guilty pleas. Saidakmetov was arrested at Kennedy Airport as he prepared to board a flight to turkey with plans to later to travel to Syria to join the terror group.

OREGON: *The headline read: "Crime career down the toilet."* A woman wanted on identity theft charges was arrested in the town of Eugene after a construction worker found her hiding beneath the lid of a portable toilet. Dawn

Shockey, 27, who had two warrants for her arrest ran when police tried to speak to her on a Saturday morning. A witness advised police that she saw the woman run through her yard and climb a fence onto the property of the Eugene Swim and Tennis club. About 20 minutes later a construction worker told police he found her after lifting the lid of a port-a-potty. Shockey voluntarily left the potty and was arrested by police. *Phew!*

PENNSYLVANIA: *Greeting cards are supposed to be given to loved ones.* Philly police are searching for a man who tried to rob a Hallmark store using a greeting card with the handwritten message inside which stated, "Give me all the money or I'll kill you." The cashier was so surprised she called over a co-worker. Then the would-be robber grabbed back the greeting card and fled.

PENNSYLVANIA: The headline read: Nails of steal." A few Sundays ago a salon worker painted a man's nails just before closing time, only to have the customer turn around, hold the workers and gunpoint and demand cash. "It's pretty nervy to sit in a nail salon and actually get a manicure and then produce a gun and announce a robbery," said Malachi Jones of the Philadelphia Police Department. The robber is still at large. Police are looking for a suspect with manicured fingernails.

PENNSYLVANIA: *He would have been better off if he had used a black beard.* Chris Furay was captured on video robbing six Pittsburgh-area banks. It has been revealed that in the first three stickups he didn't cover his real red beard. Later he disguised himself with a fake red beard. It didn't take police department to connect the dots. Furay is now in prison where he is contemplating another career he might pursue.

PENNSYLVANIA: *The headline read: "Great tackle."* Pizza –delivery man Inomjon M got car-jacked and assaulted in Pittsburgh in February by two men. The next day, his pal spotted the vehicle and alerted M, who came by in another vehicle, which the car-jackers promptly rammed. They then tried to flee on foot, but with adrenaline pumping M chased down and tackled them and held them for police.

TEXAS: *He who laughs last laughs best...* Members of a production crew, shooting footage to promote the city of Houston were robbed at gunpoint. The stick-up men took the crew's expensive equipment in front of a "We Love Houston" billboard. We learn that the crew may get the last laugh in this matter. Why? It appears that a rolling Go-Pro camera shot footage of the robbers that has been turned over to the Houston police Department.

TEXAS: *Cookie Monster, really?* Gene Bradshaw, 25, also known as "cookie monster," was arrested on a Thursday for more than 300 robberies at fast food restaurants in Texas, where he would allegedly demand cookies as well as cash. Bradshaw and his suspected accomplice, Kristy G, 25, face charges of aggravated robbery with a deadly weapon.

VIRGINIA: *What a load of bull!* Police in Mount Solon have put out an all-points bulletin after someone stole a load of bull semen. Police said 10 containers of the semen – worth up to $500 on the black market – were taken from a barn. Police also report if the thieves didn't store the semen in liquid nitrogen, it could be ruined.

WASHINGTON: *This must have been a whole lot of cupcakes!* A government employee in Yakima spent $757 of public money on fancy cupcakes for her own farewell celebration. Cheryl Mattie, the city's former human-resources director, defended the spending as legitimate. However, city officials disagree and plan to take her to small claims court to recover the $757.

WISCONSIN: *This could be hard on his love life*! A Wisconsin teenager who stole his foster parents' car and fled to Tennessee with his 16-year old girlfriend was sentenced to a year in jail by a county judge -- and then ordered not to date until his probation officer allows it. Jordan Christensen, 19, has to get permission to show a girl a good time for the three years he is on probation.

WISCONSIN: Sounds like girl gone wild. A naked bid for leniency just did not work. Julia Laack, 36, of Sheboygan was sentenced to six months in jail for shoplifting. When police went to her home, the drunken Laack stripped down to her underwear and told them they couldn't arrest her because she was naked. She eventually pleaded no contest.

WISCONSIN: *This fellow should watch CSI reruns everyday while in the slammer.* Police in La Crosse tracked down a thief who stole a tavern's safe, thanks to DNA collected from the chewing tobacco spit he left behind at the scene of the crime. A fisherman found the empty safe washed up on a sandbar in Illinois.

WISCONSIN: *Ms. Brown was too young at heart.* A Wisconsin woman allegedly stole her daughter's identity so she could go back to high school. Wendy Brown of Green Bay, enrolled in Ashwaubenon HS and joined the cheer-leading squad, attending practices and going to a pool party at the coach's house before she was caught. Brown was charged with felony ID theft.

WYOMING: *WHY?? Did they plan to open their own store?* Police report that a man and a woman recently stole more than $9,000 worth of women's undergarments from a department store. The shoplifters made off with over 1,000 Pairs of panties from a JC Penney store in Cheyenne.

Chapter Two
Thugs

A thug is defined as a violent person, especially a criminal. Thugs are usually thought of as "outlaws," who operate outside of polite society and make their living through criminal means. Historically a thug was a member of a religious cult of robbers and assassins in India. Thugs were devotees of the Hindu goddess Kali. The thugs were known to have a ritual wherein they would waylay and strangle their victims who were usually travelers. The cult was suppressed in the 1830's by the British colonials.

The word thug derives from the Hindi language word "thag" which meant a swindler or bad person. The verb thuggee in India meant the robbery and murder practiced by the thugs according to their rituals.

In America we often assume that thugs are shady and dangerous people who will do all type of untoward things for their own gain.

This chapter is about some of the dumbest modern day thugs you will ever read about. Read on.

CALIFORNIA: *You can't cut out the middle man after a murder*. A San Jose man who wanted to confess to a murder decided to cut out the middle man. So Hugh Castro, 28, turned himself in the Santa Clara County Jail. However, after he repeatedly told guards he had strangled his girlfriend, the guards transported Castro to the local police station where he was arrested.

CONNECTICUT: *She needed a spell checker on her key*. A 20-year-old woman from Stamford, who was seeking revenge on her philandering boyfriend allegedly, used a key to scratch the word "wore" into the side of the victim's vehicle. Police report. Obviously, she meant to scratch the word "whore." Nevertheless, the misspelling landed her in jail on a second-degree criminal mischief charge.

FLORIDA: *What kind of dance was it?* We learn a young man was having a good time dancing on the top of a parked Hillsborough County sheriff's police car and sipping from a bottle of brandy/ Emanuel Figueroa, 20, even spit at the deputy arresting him. Figueroa was charged with threats against a police officer and other charges.

FLORIDA: *IDIOT!!* A Florida woman was sent to jail when she called police to report being shorted by her drug dealer. Erin Klich, 36, dialed 911 in September and complained to police that she was buying marijuana in Fort Myers and was given 5.4 grams for $75, instead of the seven grams she was promised.

GEORGIA: An Atlanta man was arrested for marijuana possession after police in a patrol car caught a whiff of three 6-foot-tall weed plants he was transporting in his SUV, say police. Thomas Edwin, 38, was arrested shortly after officers detected "a strong odor of raw marijuana" coming from his Buick Rendezvous.

ILLINOIS: *The headline read: "Get in mainline."* A police raid on a heroin dealers den was interrupted when nearly a dozen people showed up looking to buy the dope, police said. In the hour and a half that the State police were at the suspected dealer's house, they located $2,300 in cash and fielded knocks on the door from 10 people who wanted to buy heroin, they said.

ILLINOIS: *Why the beef???* An impatient Wendy's drive-thru customer in Chicago was so hungry that he opened fire on another driver who tried to cut in front of him, police said. The starving suspect had pulled up in in an SUV at about 11:50 pm before the shooting unfolded. Police further reported that two men, 20 and 23, were hospitalized with injuries from broken glass.

INDIANA: *The bandits were nothing but cretins – they should have used Igor.* Interesting story. We learn if you are going to break into the Indiana Medical History Museum and steal jars of brain tissue, where can you sell it? The answer, of course, is on eBay. Police set up a sting operation to arrest David Charles, 21, and charge him with several museum break-ins. Police were tipped off by a man who had paid $670 for some of the jars of brain tissue.

LOUISIANA: *Yep, it all came out in the wash...* An accused murderer who broke out of a prison van's back window was captured after a three-day manhunt because he stopped to do his laundry. Lorenzo Conner, 24 of New Orleans, was being taken to a mental health facility when he slipped out of his shackles and fled. A tipster alerted police after spotting him at a suburban laundromat.

MICHIGAN: *The headline read: "This marijuana totally socks."* A man who brought a backpack stuffed with dirty socks to a couple looking to buy a pound of pot is facing prison time. It is reported that a fraudulent marijuana sale in Lenawee County's Raisin Township was described in court when Michael Suarez pleaded guilty to false pretenses in July 2015. The 33-year-old Suarez said he "didn't bring any weed" and instead had "a bag of dirty socks." Nevertheless, he faces up to 7 year in prison when sentenced.

MICHIGAN: *The follow-up to the previous story.* We learn that in September, Michael Suarez was sentenced to one year in jail after he was caught in July trying to sell a backpack of dirty socks as marijuana. Suarez, already a convicted felon, was using the dirty laundry to try to score $2,800 in a pot deal gone bad. We hope he will stay out of trouble with laundry after he finishes his sentence.

MICHIGAN: *You don't mess with Wendy's!* Patrons at a Wendy's drive-through in Kalamazoo got mad after their order wasn't filled to their satisfaction, so they hurled drinks, burgers and fries at a worker inside. The worker fired right back with a drink, ketchup and fries, prompting two people in the car to go inside and continue the fight with fists. The two patrons were arrested for assault.

MINNESOTA: *Good they were not fighting over the last biscuit!* He had a good reason to cry into his beer. A Minnesota man has been sentenced to five years in jail for attacking a man in a fight over the last beer in a 12-pack. The fight escalated to the point where Boonchom Soom Duangvela pulled a gun and police were forced to use a Taser to subdue him.

NEW HAMPSHIRE: *Say it ain't so Huck...* A man named Huckleberry Finn followed a woman into her home and sexually assaulted her, police say. Finn, 36, allegedly assaulted the woman in the town of Keene. The Mark Twain character's namesake was arrested shortly after the assault was reported to police. Huck was charged with sexual assault and is being held in jail in lieu of $25,000 bail.

NEW JERSEY: *Maybe Brad Pitt put them up to this!* Two day-care workers accused of running a kiddie "Fight Club" recently pleaded not guilty to charges of cruelty to children and child neglect in connection with the brawls they had children ages 4 to 6 enact at the Lightbridge Academy in the town of Cranford. It is alleged that Ms. White set up the fights and Ms. Kenny video-recorded the tussles. The videos purport to show about a dozen boys and girls shoving and striking one another during melees and one-on-one brawl on the day care playground. Kenny can allegedly be heard egging on the children and comparing the bouts to "Fight Club," as she quotes from the popular 1999 Brad

Pitt – Edward Norton movie and novel of the same name. Both women were fired and official at Lightbridge have apologized to parents.

NEW JERSEY: An atheist group, the Foundation for Freedom from Religion, tried to oppose a "Keep Christ in Christmas" banner in the town of Pitman by erecting one honoring ancient pagan rites which read "Keep Saturn in Saturnalia." However, two men in a pickup truck quickly doused it with gasoline and set it on fire.

NEW JERSEY: *Perhaps she was a Houdini relative!* A Georgia resident was one of several suspects arrested at a Walmart in Union City for alleged credit card fraud. She was handcuffed behind her back and left alone in the rear of a police car while officers tended to the other suspects. Somehow the 5-foot-seven, 140-pound lady managed to get her hands in front of her, climb through the small partition between the front and back sets and sped off. Police continue to search for her.

NEW YORK: *The poor defendant was punished even before the trial ended!* An upstate New York Judge declared a mistrial a day after two jurors on their lunch hour witnessed the gun-rap defendant in their case get beaten with a chair outside a doughnut shop. Jerome Johnson was attacked around 1 pm at a Dunkin' Donuts across the street from the Rensselaer County courthouse in Troy, according to a news report. Johnson suffered a concussion and was transported to a local hospital, his lawyer claims. The two jurors expressed that they could no longer continue with the case and a mistrial was declared because only twelve jurors and one alternate had been seated.

NEW YORK: *The headline read: "The suspect was no wiz."* It has been reported that a Brooklyn man police suspected of public urination was a 26-year-old who shot himself in the groin as he tried to hide his handgun from officers who thought he was relieving himself. Patrol officers spotted Javier Thomas at 1:00 am near a street corner with his back to them. Believing he was reliving himself the officers approached. However, Thomas was actually re-positioning his loaded Glock 19 he was carrying. Upon seeing the officers he tried to yank the gun from his trousers and in his haste he accidentally pulled the trigger. The maimed Thomas tried to limp away from the scene but was caught by the police. They recovered the gun and Thomas has been charged with reckless endangerment and criminal possession of a weapon.

NEW YORK CITY: *What a sting for a crossing guard, and it wasn't even real coke!* An on-duty crossing guard in Queens was arrested after being given a bag with cash and cocaine inside and failing to turn it in to law enforcement authorities. Bernard Pelzer, 58, was directing school children across the street when he was targeted in an NYPD integrity test designed to nab department employees for misconduct. He took a bag containing cash and white powder that looked like cocaine and tried to keep it. He was charged with petit larceny, official misconduct, possession of stolen property and possession of a controlled substance. *Silly Pelzer, he should have smelled a set up.*

MASSACHUSETTS: *One word: NITWITS!* Three men in Springfield held up a food-delivery driver at knifepoint and tried to make off with his car. One problem! None of the dummies knew how to drive a stick-shift vehicle. After grinding the gears for a few minutes, the three ran down the street with the food order.

MASSACHUSSETTS: *Misdeeds in the drug trade??* A mixed-martial-arts fighter was arrested for allegedly beating two men he strapped to a cross. Vito Resto of Springfield hung his victims on the makeshift cross and pummeled them for "misdeeds in the drug trade," reports say. Resto, a top fighter who has a tattoo of Christ on one shoulder, pleaded not guilty to kidnapping, assault and battery charges.

MASSACHUSETTS: *The headline read: "A real hoot!"* A drunken driver smashed his car into a snowbank, drove off with police on his tail, then jumped over a guardrail and ran into some woods. Police spotted him an hour later – 30 feet up in a tree he had climbed. The man asked the police had they caught the "guy who had crashed." Then he explained it could not have been him because he was an owl.

MISSOURI: *This one will probably be dismissed very soon.* A couple was arrested for shooting a fast-food drive-through clerk -- with a Nerf gun. Stephanie W 22, and Mark A, 26 were charged with assault despite not causing any injuries with the stunt caught on surveillance video in suburban St. Louis.

NEVADA: *Her attorney says she will fight the charges! I say there's not a chance she'll win.* Last year a Vegas pet shop owner who prosecutors contend was seen on security cameras torching her store with 27 puppies inside was handcuffed and taken to jail. The judge in the case set her bail at $250,000 which made her stay in jail for quite some time before trial. Animal rights activist protested the bail set for Hye Lee and a new judge in the case raised the bail to $310,000. Although Lee has been charged with felony burglary and arson charges, fire fighters were able to rescue all the pups that were not harmed.

NEW YORK CITY: *What kind of thug wears a teddy-bear hat to an armed robbery?* A man dressed in a teddy-bear hat and armed with a large knife tried to rob a woman in the lobby of her Manhattan building. The 31-year-old victim had just exited a subway station when the suspect started trailing her. When she entered the lobby of her building he followed her inside, pulled a butcher knife and demanded her purse and valuables. She fought him off and he fled. NYPD put out a look out for the suspect described as being about 25 years old, 5-foot-5 and 130 pounds, who was last seen wearing beige knitted teddy-bear hat and a camouflage jacket.

NEW YORK CITY: *Angel, you are a dangerous blockhead!* Angel Flores, 47, went ballistic because he did not like the photos of him that his girlfriend had posted to her Facebook. He demanded that she take the photos down. When she did not do so right away, he grabbed her

2-year-old daughter and threatened to throw her from the 10th-floor balcony of the girlfriend's Staten Island apartment. He then pulled a knife on the girlfriend and next ripped a television off a wall and stomped it to bits. Police were called. The woman and child were not seriously injured and Flores was arrested for criminal mischief, weapon possession and endangering the life of a child.

TEXAS: *Tinkle, tinkle little star…* Daniel Athens, 23, of El Paso must pay a $4,000 fine and could have faced up to 10 months in jail after pleading guilty to urinating on the Alamo – a felony crime! Athens was tackled by a member of the Alamo rangers after ducking under a barrier chain in front of the San Antonio landmark to get close enough to urinate on the façade.

WISCONSIN: *This guy is nut job and a pervert!* A Wisconsin man says his religious beliefs stopped him from murdering and raping women…but that apparently didn't prevent him from breaking into their homes, stealing their underwear and sending them threatening notes. Christopher Sullivan, 43, is accused of sending some of the women pictures of decapitated Barbie dolls, along with messages that they would be likewise treated and "we will have your skull at our table of sacrifice."

Chapter Three
Rogues

Although many people cannot define the word rogue, most people know a rogue when they meet one. The word rogue is defined as a dishonest or unprincipled man. Another definition of a rogue is that of a person whose behavior one disapproves of but who is nonetheless likable or attractive. Finally, a rogue is also defined as a person or thing that behaves in an aberrant, faulty or unpredictable way.

You will find many rogues in this chapter that certainly fit this final definition because they act in dumb, aberrant ways that are often faulty and/or unpredictable.

Enjoy!

ARIZONA: *OH POO*... A state lawmaker wants to hit undocumented immigrants where it hurts: in the bathroom. State Rep. Carl Steel has sponsored a bill that would make it a felony for anyone illegally in the U.S. to use a public restroom. The bill would also ban them from using sidewalks and roads. The proposal has made a number of pro-immigrant groups so angry that they presented Steel with a toilet with his face painted on it.

CALIFORNIA: *Me Tarzan – You Jane*... A man who claimed to be Tarzan was arrested after he climbed a tree and tried to get into a zoo's monkey exhibit, authorities said. The shirtless man plastered in mud had climbed about 20 feet into tree at the bird exhibit at Santa Ana Zoo. He was apparently high on meth police said when they arrested him.

CONNECTICUT: *Nope – no good deed goes unpunished.* A man is accused of kidnapping and feeding a man he thought was homeless. David Pope was arrested after he tried to take a 77-year-old man he had seen in Danbury pushing a cart of cans and bottles. Despite refusing his advances, Pope grabbed the man by the arm and forced him back to his house. After being fed by Pope and bit by a pit bull, the man escaped and called police.

CONNECTICUT: Wh*y should they practice what they preach??* We recently learned that the Fire Department headquarters in New London, Conn, does not meet fires-safety codes according to an investigative report. The building has no fire alarm or sprinkler system according to the report. The building is also filled with rodents. "Yes, we have mice. Doesn't everyone?" the fire chief told reporters at a press conference.

FLORIDA: *The first shall be last and the last shall be first, maybe?* A Lake County corrections officer recently agreed to a plea agreement that will give him 15 years in a federal prison. Why? Greed. In early 2015 officer Robert Brown, 32, allegedly began smuggling contraband into the Coleman Federal Correctional complex in Sumter County in exchange for cash. Federal agents began monitoring Brown's action after an inmate told officials that Brown was providing cellphones, tobacco, synthetic marijuana and unknown pills to him. Agents soon set up a sting between Brown and a cooperating witness. In the sting Brown was caught accepting $2,600 in exchange for contraband. When confronted by the agents Brown confessed he had illegally negotiated $7,100 in cash payments in return for smuggling cellphones, tobacco, drugs and other items to inmates.

FLORIDA: *XXX*... We learn that a High-schooler is fighting expulsion after local education officials discovered information about his after school job – acting in adult films. Robert M said Cocoa High School had no right to expel him from school because he legally performed as an 18-year-old and he did the work off campus.

FLORIDA: *The headline read simply: "Locker shocker"* A man who called for help when he fell and was injured at his Orlando storage unit ended up in the Orange County Jail after the police noticed that the man was storing decades-old child pornography. Fleet Peeples, 76, of Casselberry was arrested and police then searched for children in the images which are believed to now be between 30 to 50 years old.

FLORIDA: *The headline read: "Practice makes perfect."* It has been reported that a South Florida man who swallowed 115 pellets of cocaine told police he had been smuggling coke for years. Matthew Lawson, 32, admitted "transporting cocaine internally for four years." He stated, further that he started with just 15 pellets and worked his way up to higher amounts." according to police. He also admitted that he had made about 15 successful practice trips from Jamaica to the United States.

FLORIDA: *Felonious sea turtle riding arrest?* A 20-year-old young lady, who allegedly was caught sitting or riding on sea turtles in photos that went viral on social media, was arrested in September by Melbourne police. Stephanie Moore, one of two women photographed sitting on or riding sea turtles, was wanted on a felony warrant in connection with the alleged conduct. The photos that went viral prompted numerous complaints to the Florida Fish and wildlife Conservation Commission. Ms. Moore now sits in the Brevard County jail awaiting a bail hearing.

FLORIDA: *...And they say honesty is always the best policy – HA!* A woman tried to hit her husband with her car after he confessed to a four-decades-old affair. Barbara Yedynak, 77, was so enraged at the confession that she threatened to the husband with a knife and scratched too, before trying to hit him with her car.

FLORIDA: *CHOMP!* A 32-year-old man was arrested and charged with aggravated battery in august after authorities said he bit off the tip of a woman's middle finger after she waved it in his face during an argument. Hillsborough sheriff deputies responded to a battery call and found the woman lying on a lawn chair, a half-inch of her finger was missing. She underwent surgery to repair the wound authorities said. Christopher Butler of Seffner was arrested the same night as his home. When Butler was arrested he was so intoxicated he could not stand on his own. He was transported to jail and faces a charge of aggravated battery with great bodily harm, a felony.

FLORIDA: *The headline for this read: "Dope and change."* Mayor Carlos Hernandez, the Mayor of Hialeah tried to pay a $4,000 city ethics fine with 360,000 pennies and nickels – 28 buckets of coins in all. Since the city ethics commission says he knew it only accepted checks they doubled his fine. Now the Mimi-Dade Commission on Ethics and Public Trust is suing Mayor Hernandez.

IOWA: *OMG! "Poopsenders.com"* A woman experiencing bad blood between her and her neighbors is facing a stint in jail after mailing them a box of cow dung. We learn that Kim Cape, 41, used "poopsenders.com" to anonymously mail the dung to the neighboring couple after they repeatedly complained to police about her dog's barking. "After all the problems we've had, I thought it would be a funny thing to do," Cape explained to authorities.

MICHIGAN: *The revenge of the nerd!* A 17 year old allegedly having a sexual relationship with his teacher at Freeland High School in Saginaw turned in his teacher when he suspected she was cheating on him with the assistant principal. The assistant principal resigned and the teacher is on trial for sexual assault.

MICHIGAN: A state lawmaker was expelled and another quit in mid-September, 2015 over their attempt to hide their affair with a bogus, sexually explicit email. Rep. Cindy Gamrat, 42, was voted out just after 4 am during a legislative session. Rep Todd Courser, 43, who also faced expulsion had resigned and hour earlier. Courser admitted sending out a graphic email in May contending he was caught with a male prostitute. It was intended to distract from the affair. Gamrat admitted that she had discussed the plot with him.

MICHIGAN: *D'OH!* A reserve police officer was arrested after allegedly showing up to a sex-for drugs exchange in his police uniform. It appears that Mike Strong of Prairieville Township Police Department did not realize that it might have been a bad idea to bring his service revolver along with him when he went to meet a man he believed would give him sexual favors in exchange for illegal substances. Unfortunately, Strong was actually meeting Michigan State police investigators who promptly arrested him in a sting operation. *D'OH!*

MICHIGAN: *Mr. Senior citizen beats jail time in Grand Rapids! They were probably worried that they would be responsible for his health care there.* Howard Klein, 87, was arrested for allegedly soliciting a prostitute who was really an undercover police officer. Kent County D.A. William Forsyth said there would be nothing gained by jailing Klein and declined to press charges against the codger. Forsyth said, "He shouldn't go to jail after 87 years without involvement in the criminal justice system, in my opinion, he earned a pass."

MINNESOTA: *What a weirdo...Talk about a deflation fetish.* Police are searching for a Duluth man who gets turned on by slashing big rubber exercise balls at gyms. The 31 year old man, who is well known to law enforcement, was caught on tape cutting 70 rubber balls. He has been arrested for this before and told cops he lusts after inflatable devices.

NEW HAMPSHIRE: *Remember this is the Live Free or Die State! This action doesn't sound like living free!* We learn that this state has recently recalled 500 books of cocktail recipes that the state had printed and distributed to state-run liquor stores. Why? A state Liquor Commission spokesperson said the guides should have been vetted more closely to omit drink names including "Stripper Mom," "Busted Rubber" and "Panty Dropper."

NEW YORK: *No niceness for a wannabe ISIS thug!* A Buffalo judge has denied bail for a western New York man accused of attempting to support terrorism by buying combat gear, making overseas trips and declaring his allegiance online to ISIS. A federal judge in August agreed with the government that Arafat Nagi is too much of a flight risk and too dangerous to the community to be released following his arrest at his Lackawanna home. The case is now headed to a grand jury.

NORTH CAROLINA: *Mo money, mo jail time...* A college student in Greensboro was arrested in January for counterfeiting after allegedly passing phony $100 bills bearing the signature "Moe Money" instead of that of the Secretary of the Treasury. Symone Brown had allegedly produced nearly $13,000 in "Moe" bills.

NORTH CAROLINA: *OOOUUCCHH!!* A 51-year-old resident has been charged with assault and malicious castration after she bit her boyfriend's testicles during a domestic dispute. The police report reveals that the alleged victim required eight stitches, but suffered no long term damage.

OREGON: *A mother's job is never done.* A mother was sentenced to 30 days in jail for trying to smuggle contraband – meth and oxycodone – behind bars to her incarcerated daughter. The daughter, doing a four year stretch for identity theft, was given another eight months for the attempted smuggle.

PENNSYLVANIA: *Police "liked" him on Facebook.* Anthony Lescow, who was wanted on a warrant for assault, got cocky and posted the police department wanted poster of him on his Facebook page. That's when an attractive woman coaxed Lescow to meet him for a cigarette. Yep, you guessed it! There was no attractive woman meeting him – just a team of undercover officers who promptly arrested him based on the warrant.

PENNSYLVANIA: *Evil twin??* A man in this state tried to get out of robbery charges by contending his "evil twin" committed the crimes. Steve Felton, 34, used a pellet gun to rob ten gas stations in Allentown. Unfortunately, his "evil twin" defense did not work. It is now reported that a judge sentenced him to 62 to 124 years in state prison.

PENNSYLVANIA: *She's sorry -- but he still be dead!* It has been reported that a woman in the town of Erie who fatally punched a 63-year-old named Paris

Hilton, faces up to five years in prison. Sandra Gray maintains Hilton made unwanted sexual advances toward her. She pleaded guilty to involuntary manslaughter before an Erie County judge. Her defense attorney says Gray didn't mean to kill him.

PENNSYLVANIA: A man allegedly pummeled his big brother for eating three Big Mac sandwiches without saving him a single bite. Thomas Veres, 47, was charged with simple assault and harassment after he attached Matthew, 58, at their home in Union Township. The starving sibling bruised his brother's right eye and left cheek, according to the police report.

VIRGINIA: *Johnny Reb, your side lost!* A man is in hot water with police over his Confederate-flag license plates. "I will go to jail before I change those tags," said Kevin Collier, who is described as a loud and proud good ol' boy. He refuses to remove his sons of Confederate Veterans license plate even though state lawmakers voted to ban the Confederate tags, which on October 4, 2015 became invalid

VIRGINIA: *Arachnophobia??* A state prosecutor is in trouble. Why? He went to a Halloween office party that was decorated for the holiday and included a goodly number of plastic spiders. Logan County assistant prosecutor Chris White, who has a severe arachnophobia, freaked out upon seeing the spiders. He pulled out a handgun and threatened to shoot them. Although no one was hurt, Mr. White was suspended indefinitely.

WASHINGTON, D.C.: *The fox should not guard the chicken coop!* Fueled by an addiction to prescription painkillers, an FBI agent abused heroin from his own drug investigations and in the process ruined dozens of cases involving suspected drug traffickers according to details that recently emerged. Matthew Lowery, formerly a special agent with the Washington field office, will plead guilty to 64 charges of obstruction of justice, heroin possession and conversion of property.

WISCONSIN: *Yes, the answer is yes...he was drunk!* This may or may not be what they mean by marking your territory, Torey Devaux, a Wisconsin man, sought revenge on his roommate who refused to have sex with him by peeing on her dog. Devaux then shoved the woman's sister into a wall and punched out a window.

Chapter Four

Thieves, Thugs, & Rogues from Abroad

My last chapter are stories from abroad. Now that you know the definitions of thieves, thugs and rogues I will leave it to you, the readers to decide who in these stories may be the thieves, who are the thugs and who are the rogues.

I hope you get a few laughs as you do so.

BRAZIL: It is well known that prisoners have no use for "rats." However, mice are different. It has been reported that inmates of a Brazilian prison used a mouse as a drug mule after training it to go from cell to cell with a packet of cocaine on its tail.

CANADA: *Busted for the lack of a bell and more*! Police in Edmonton pulled over a cyclist to cite him for riding on the sidewalk and not having a bell on his bike. During the stop, a knife fell out of the 25-year-old's pants and an ensuing search turned up a sawed off shotgun and drugs in his backpack. Police say he is now facing weapons and drug charges along with a ticket for not having a bell on his bike.

CANADA: *The headline read: "Later gators."* A Toronto couple turned their home into a makeshift reptile sanctuary, harboring more than 150 crocodiles, alligators and caimans inside for the past

10 years. "I couldn't believe what I was seeing," said Bry Loyst, of the Indian River Reptile Zoo, after he was called in by police last August.

CHINA: *Free Airport Eats?* A Chinese man found that you could get a free lunch if you ate at the airport. The man managed to scam months' worth of free meals in the VIP lounge at the Xi'an Airport in Shaanxi by buying a first class ticket, and then switching his flight to the next day after he ate. The man continued to switch the flight over and over until the ticket expired, when he just cancelled it.

CHINA: *Should we assume he was not a morning person?* A man in China beat up his mother and broke four of her ribs after she refused to bring him breakfast in bed. The 27-year-old suspect has been arrested by police.

CHINA: *This was not the last stand of the mighty 300!* Several scantily clad men, marching in formation like Spartan warriors, were thrown down by Beijing police during a restaurant's ill-fated publicity stunt. The men, in skimpy leather shorts, sandals and capes marched with plastic containers of salad to hype the restaurant Sweetie Salad. Police arrested several of the salad Spartans, saying such gatherings must be approved in advance.

ENGLAND: *The headline read: "Being an incorrigible rogue is no longer illegal."* The British Ministry of Justice reported that the offense, created in the early 19th century, was one of more than 300 obsolete offenses which have been abolished over the past year. The legislative history reveals that the 1824 Vagrancy Act was passed to deter and punish "idle and disorderly persons." The law defined an "incorrigible rogue" as a homeless person who resisted arrest or escaped confinement. Oh so British!

ENGLAND: *He really "nailed" this job!* A British house builder had to be rescued from the roof of a home in the city of Essex in October after he nailed his hand to a wooden rafter. The unnamed 30-year-old had been using a high powered nail gun at the time of the accident. The woebegone man spent 45 minutes on the roof before he was rescued by firefighters.

ENGLAND: *What, pray do tell, is fish pornography???* Nelson Nazare, 45, was ordered to spend six weeks in jail after he was caught with fish-abuse pornography on his phone. The St. Neots resident was originally arrested for harassing his wife but police later found the pornography and tacked on charges for possessing the extreme images.... *Fish pornography???*

ENGLAND: *Dicey spicy?* Four homes in Manchester had to be evacuated after a neighbor cooking an extremely spicy chili sent caustic fumes throughout the neighborhood. A group of college students getting ready for a Halloween party thought there was a gas leak when they rushed outside because of the toxic air, only to find their neighbor apologizing to everyone in the neighborhood.

ENGLAND: *Hog wild, maybe??* Police who were asked to check on the welfare of folks living in a house in suburban England found a menagerie – including a fully grown pig, three dogs, four ferrets and 12 cats. The owner of the animals, a 41-year-old woman, was later arrested for threatening a woman she believed had called the police about her four legged pets.

ENGLAND: *Take photos of yourself in your garden? Maybe not!* A British man, Richard Edmunds, took a selfie photo of himself in his garden. Unfortunately, his garden was an indoor grow house full of marijuana plants. Shortly after taking the selfie British police found a copy of the photo during a raid. Mr. Edmunds is now in jail.

ENGLAND: *She must have not been much of a girlfriend!* A man was arrested for having sex with his girlfriend's dog after she discovered a cell phone video of him doing the deed with the dog. The 19-year-old perv admitted to having sex with the bull terrier after the girlfriend took his phone to the police station and showed the footage. Upon his arrest police found him in possession of marijuana.

ENGLAND: *The wet work did not work.* A man who allegedly stole money from a charity fountain in the town of Wells initially denied that he had taken anything when police stopped and questioned him – but piles of soggy coins gave him away. "He then started to run away and wet, loose change flew out of his pockets and onto the pavement," inspector mark Nicholson said.

ENGLAND: *The headline read: "This guy is facing some hard time."* Authorities say they got a rise when they discovered an illicit stash of half a million pills for erectile dysfunction in a house in suburban London. They arrested the 37-year-old man there for possessing unauthorized medication

ENGLAND: *The "beast of the bedroom has now been caged."* A British man with a lot to boast about in the bedroom telephoned emergency services 30 times in four hours just to brag. The 59-year-old called the hotline to tell of his prowess in bed. Officials traced the calls and arrested the suspect for wasting police resources. He is now in jail.

ENGLAND: *He admits he was a bad buoy*. A former Royal Navy sailor admitted in court to stealing piles of water-resistant clothing because he has a fetish for the slippery material. "I get sexual gratification out of the feeling of the waterproof clothing on my skin," Alan Reynolds, 55 of Cornwall, told a judge. "I know it is irrational and I am sorry."

ENGLAND: A British grandmother says thieves in the night made off with 90 square feet of her perfectly manicured $4,000 artificial lawn in Wrexham. Police are now searching for the snake in the grass, who they believe sneaked onto the property after dark, rolled up squares of the lawn and fled.

ENGLAND: He was clocked with his own clock! A drunken wife gave a new meaning to getting "clocked in the head" when she bashed her husband with their bedside alarm clock. Monty Borthwick,

59, of Portsmouth was getting ready for bed when he turned to his wife, Kathryne, and asked her for a good night kiss. She responded by beating him with the clock. A judge slapped her with a yearlong community service sentence.

FRANCE: *He should count his blessings and not sue.* A Frenchman who has been getting paid more than $5,500 a month to stay home from work for more than ten years now wants over $500,000 in compensation because he claimed his career is ruined. Charles Simon revealed a short time ago that he is asking to be compensated for the 12 years he spent doing absolutely nothing after his bosses suspended him with pay in 2003.

NORWAY: *Surf was up so he hung ten…* A Norwegian prisoner used a surfboard to escape from an island prison. Bastoy Prison is praised for its humane treatment of inmates, who are taught organic farming and are allowed to go cycling on the beach. The prison chief indicated to the prisoner's family that once the escapee is captured, he will be shipped to a less luxurious facility when he said: "There is no return ticket if you run away."

SCOTLAND: *Yes, he really had to go...* A driving instructor led police on a 120-mph chase because he was desperate to get to a toilet. The 49-year-old man stepped on the gas after seeing police and then frantically pulled into a diner. He later claimed he sped up not to evade police – but because he didn't want to "soil himself" while driving.

SCOTLAND: It was reported that in early October hungry thieves made off with nearly $70,000 of Kellogg's breakfast bars. The thieves apparently snuck a tractor-trailer container with nearly 20,000 pounds of the cereal snacks out of a Lockerbie parking area sometime around 2:30 am on a Thursday morning.

None of the snack bars have turned up and no arrests have been made.

SAUDI ARABIA: *Seems someone was planning a big beer bash!* Saudi customs authorities discovered 48,000 cans of illegal beer disguised as Pepsi and being smuggled into the country. Video shows customs officers cutting off the blue cola label to find green-and-white Heineken cans underneath. Importation or brewing of beer or the distilling and selling of any alcohol product is against the law in Saudi Arabia.

SPAIN: *The headline read: Small town, "monumental error."* Local authorities in the town of San Cristovo de Cea thought that they were giving the town of 2,400 a little rehab when they replaced a few moss covered rocks with a new picnic bench – only to ignite the furor of history lovers. The so-called "bureaucratic blockheads" claim they had no idea that they removed stones placed there 6,000 years ago by some of Spain's first inhabitants to mark a prehistoric tomb.

The End

About the Author

Professor Birdsong received his J.D. from the Harvard Law School and his B.A. from Howard University. He teaches law in Orlando, Florida.

After graduation from law school he worked four years at the law firm of Baker Hostetler. He then entered into a varied and distinguished career in government service. He served as a diplomat with the U.S. State Department with various postings in Nigeria, Germany and the Bahamas.

Professor Birdsong later served as a federal prosecutor. After leaving government service, and before he began teaching, Professor Birdsong was in private law practice in Washington, D.C.

www.BirdsongsLaw.com

lbirdsong@barry.edu

Ordering Information

New books coming soon!

Dear Reader,

If you liked this book, I would greatly appreciate you writing me a review on Amazon or any other book site.

I look forward to sharing more funny stories with you in future books.

Thank you, I really appreciate your help.

Regards,

Professor Birdsong

Winghurst Publications
1969 S. Alafaya Trail / Suite 303
Orlando, FL 32828-8732
www.BirdsongsLaw.com
lbirdsong@barry.edu

Other Books by Professor Birdsong:

* Professor Birdsong's 147 Dumbest Criminal Stories: Florida.

* 177 Dumbest Criminal Stories – International.

* Professor Birdsong's 157 Dumbest Criminal Stories.

* Professor Birdsong's Weird Criminal Law Stories.

* Professor Birdsong's "365" Weird Criminal Law Stories for Every Day of the Year.

* Professor Birdsong's Weird Criminal Law Stories, Volume 2: Stories From Around the States and Abroad.

* Professor Birdsong's Weird Criminal Law Stories, Volume 3: Stories from New York City and the East Coast.

* Professor Birdsong's Weird Criminal Law Stories - Volume 4: Stories from the Midwest.

* Professor Birdsong's Weird Criminal Law Stories, Volume 5: Stories from Way Out West.

* Professor Birdsong's Weird Criminal Law Stories - Volume 6: Women in Trouble.

* Professor Birdsong's Weird Criminal Law - Volume 6: Women in Trouble!

* Immigration: Obama must act now!

* Professor Birdsong's 77 Dumbest Criminal Stories.

* Professor Birdsong's Dumbest: Thugs, Thieves, and Rogues.

Leonard Birdsong